Life in the Condo

THE SENIOR VERSION

Alice Bowen Gibson

ISBN 978-1-64471-455-3 (Paperback)
ISBN 978-1-64471-456-0 (Digital)

Covenant Books, Inc.
11661 Hwy 707
Murrells Inlet, SC 29576
www.covenantbooks.com

To Tom, who said with a smile,
"That's one for the book!"

Illustrations by Jacqui Blatchford
Edits by Monica Becker
Photo by James Mars

Contents

What Is a Condo?

*W*hat, after all, is a condo?

We hear this word *condo* bantered about almost daily and as part of most vocabularies. It sounds old, maybe ancient, in fact. Is it Latin? Roman? Or Greek? They invented everything, didn't they?

I remember in grade school reading about cliff dwellers and seeing pictures in our *Weekly Reader* of the cliffs with ladders and stick figures near the doors. It must be forever that humans have lived under the same roofs, came out of their doors each morning to greet the world of their neighbors. Neighbor. Maybe that's it— crowding together, herd mentality, feeling safe, and not doing it alone. Home alone? Maybe not!

However, a little reading tells that although some corporate or co-op type of housing or apartments, were in our history, it was not until 1960 in the United States that joint yet individual ownership of property devised, and later, changes were made to the National Housing Act to ensure mortgages on condominium properties.

The word condominium itself or versions of it have been around forever, it seems—being found on Europe, buildings, and in Roman ruins. It is most probably of Latin derivation.

What is the difference between a condo/townhouse, condo/co-op, condo/villa, condo/apartment, condo/duplex, condo/single-family? Okay?

Already got it! A condo is in the ownership.

Bottom line, a condo is a collection of individual home units, common area, and land. The boundaries of the individual space, specified by a legal document and recorded plus interest in the common areas, comprise the type of ownership. The condo owner receives a title, can sell the unit on the market, just as other real property may be bought and sold. Laws govern the real property. Rules of the condo association apply to all owners equally. The condo associ ation declaration becomes the guiding principle to follow.

So, why in the world would someone, anyone, buy into such ownership?

The Decision
to Buy One

*W*ell, the reasons are many!

Maybe a desire to try something new—everyone knows someone who has done it! Sold the old house, kicked up their heels, bought a "condo," moved to "Sun City" somewhere, became young again, did young things like dance lessons (the Congo maybe), swim lessons, learned woodworking, golf, exercises (even from a chair), ceramic classes, book groups, travel excursion to Zam-bi-a? (where is that?), love safaris, make big albums of animal pictures (thought they might meet a Robert Redford, like in *Out of Africa!*). If only! I don't know why they did it! Or maybe someone found themselves alone and single after a hundred years of waking up each morning with the same spouse, asking, "What are we going to do today?" The other grunts. "Ugh! That's enough!" It was just too hard to think of "forever alone." Maybe the thought of other humans making noises, banging on pipes, moving about was attractive—anything but the sad silence. Maybe sell the house, be a part of something. Maybe the security of not jumping at every creaking chair or shudder at 3:00 a.m. and imagining that some stranger, without question, was going to appear! Yikes!

Change? Maybe that was it! Long years of nine to five, shower at 6:00 a.m. to get ready for the trip to the airport, gut-wrenching fear that you don't have a new sale to talk about at the morning sales meeting (everyone else will have one!). And there will be a silence when it's your turn! You just know that Jim guy will have one! And you aren't old enough for Social Security and Medicare. The bills will arrive on the fifteenth and thirtieth! Have to stay put! Then again, maybe it is time to "downsize." That's the new word, isn't it?

Call the realtor, pray for a buyer, find a condo! Salvation is at hand! Think again! Where to go?

Wasn't there a new development in town? New condos—bright, shiny, exotic (like the pictures in *Architecture Digest*), condos coming on the market! Why not—"me too"? I'm not too old, am I? And the money—hey ya! Think of all the savings! Lower taxes (maybe), no lawn care, no snow removal, no tree care, no roof repairs, no drains to unplug, no painters! Yeah! Save, save, monthly assessments? Well, yes, but just one bill—a piece of cake! Call the realtor!

So convinced! Take the condo tours.

Wow! Are they really that small? My favorite couch? Won't fit anywhere? Can you really do laundry in that space? Yeah! There is a pool; that should be fun! Have to buy a new swim-suit (a bikini?—well, maybe not!). Have to clear up that toe fungus and slim that belly! (Always something to drive you nuts!) Dad was right when he always said that!

Are the halls really that long? I don't know! Looks like a motel? Never lived with an elevator to go "home." Better look at first-floor units—visions of screaming from a third-floor balcony—five alarms ringing, a handsome fire-fighter calling, "Jump!" into a net (just like in the movies!). Am I playacting? Would this be me? Could this be me? Each night, each morning? What happens when people really cook, and the smell of pot roast or meat loaf wafts down the hall? Or better yet, fish! Then heaven forbid if someone smokes, and all end up with coughs or something worse! Or what about that guy walking through the hall that had a big patch on his uniform:

"Exterminator"? Ek, ek, ek! What "vermins" inhabit the place? And who runs these condos? Boards! What's that? Who pays the bills? Who calls the service people? Who manages? Maybe the smoke alarms go off in the middle of the night? Then what?

Ponder! Ponder! Ponder! Decision time!

Like the sound of hooves coming around the corner in the Wild West, Gary Cooper movies, help is on the way! Giddyap! Giddyap! Imagine—a REALTOR just called! Just checking in the neighborhood, has a buyer looking for a house just like yours, wants to get in before school starts. Have you ever thought about selling the house? They are sitting outside in the car!

Is this manna from heaven or just the devil himself tempting you with various ways for you to sell your soul? Put you out on the street—homeless, hungry, losing weight, a spectacle for the neighborhood? All of one's earthly goods in a shopping cart from Jewel? Well, maybe it would be a good idea to just try to see what the market would be? Figures start forming in the cerebellum? Is that where the numbers stay in the brain? Or is it the whatever "campus" part of the left or right gray matter? Anyway, it's perc-o-lating up there! If not today, someday! Why not give it a try? If the offer is too low, you can always say "no thanks" and wait for another! Can't you? Golly, never thought it would really work! Maybe it won't. The old house is not so bad, can stay a little longer—isn't this the one we built? The "dream house" where the kids called it HOME! Where the yellow school bus stopped that first day of kindergarten, and the five-year-old (the baby) got on after watching so many times when her best friend got on, and now it was finally her turn. Isn't this the place the chocolate chips were baked, birthday parties were held, graduation diplomas were displayed on the bookcase— where Gramma came for Christmas with her box of chocolates (she had to bring it, or she was told she would have to go back on the bus)! Where "sick chicks" were cared for with Vicks and vaporizers, where Dad was cheered and kissed on

Friday when he danced in the doorway announcing a new sale that week. Where young 'uns grew big and ventured away to learn of life in foreign lands.

What will anyone else see? Oh! I know! They'll see bricks and mortar, tight Pella windows, microwaves, refrigerators, square footage, room sizes, paint colors, furnaces, patios, baths, and Jacuzzi tubs! *Not at all what I see!*

They won't see the fireplaces at Christmas and hear the snapping of the burning logs, Sunday dinners, the broken dish that was your favorite, the dog that pranced on Christmas morning for baloney slices, thrown out with cheers and laughter, the hellos, the goodbyes, the daily chores, the electricity outage, the new carpeting, the flooded basement when the sump pump failed, the letter that came from church camp that the ten-year-old was attending, explaining that she was writing during chapel and the minister was preaching on "salvation," but she wasn't listening because she knew all about that already! Then the football game! The broken leg! That it hurt so much to watch, that it seemed as if your leg (maybe both of them) was being broken too!

The habitat of duties at hand and deferred, the smiling neighbors and friends that opened the front door for visits, for cups of tea, for holiday open houses!

What are you thinking? Could you really sell? When the chips are down? You, who resist change? You, who really think things will stay the same? You, who cry saying goodbye to a cat? You, who inherited your mother's sentimentality and said every time you had to leave home, "Some things don't get better with practice."

Then the phone rings—it is the realtor! She wants to show the house! People are out front and want to see inside, love the neighborhood. Well, well, should I? Or shouldn't I? Advantages, disadvantages? Make a mental checklist (like Ben Franklin used to do, plus and minus)! Why not? No certainty they will even like it, let alone want to buy it!

Okay! Hurry to hang up the towels in the bathroom. Flush! Flush! Check the kitchen sink for dishes. Check! Beds made? Okay there, the doorbell rings. Golly! That was fast (I was just going to wash the kitchen floor when the phone rang!).

You go outside, just checking the backyard as the realtor does her thing. Your heart beats a little faster. Oh, golly, you didn't have time to check the refrigerator. Do they really look inside? And my closet!

Ekk!

It takes forever (wasn't it only seven days to create the whole world?). The

door slams, the car motor
starts, they are gone!

Whew! I come inside.
Has there been a "home
invasion"? What did they
think? Did they hate my
paint choices? (I know
that carpet needs clean-
ing!) Well, they didn't give
much notice (ten minutes,
maybe), did they?

What did they expect? I
didn't want to sell anyway!
They'll be sorry. They just
saw a house! They have
no idea of the memories:
the living here, the joys,
the tears, the hugs, and
the no-speaking days, the
mad-as-hell days, the are-

you-still-crazy-about-me days (wonder if he still is; he used to say that he was!), the LOVE days—no further thoughts.

Back to "life before the realtor." Okay, okay, I know! I know! Those people, "THOSE PEOPLE," put in an offer. Too good to turn down. Yes. It's true; we have a closing date. A real, exact calendar date that is marked in red—moving day!

The Move

$\mathcal{A}$ll the details, all the jumping around, can't sleep, too many lists.

To do list:

1. Call the moving company
2. Get boxes
3. Newspapers for wrapping
4. Utility companies (Nightmare there. Will

I ever have a working telephone again? Want the same number; everyone knows it for sure.)

Did we really do this? Where will we live? Have no address. Panic. Panic. Just remembered that a friend from church said so and so might move because wife was ill, needed to live closer to daughter in another state. Great! What's his number?

First thing! Called him! And yes, he just might if he could get the right price! (Oh! Oh! That means it will

be high with no negotia-
tion!) He held all the cards;
it was the only possibil-
ity right now. First floor
(wanted that), good loca-
tion in the building, pool
view. Could close when we
could. He hadn't done anything to the condo, even
unpacked all the boxes.
But he was a "mechanical
nut." His profession was
fixing/straightening teeth,
had even fixed the teeth
of a princess of some little country once, maybe
Pakistan. Everything had to
work, all new appliances,
but (there's always a *but*,
isn't there?) only two bed-

rooms (no den, wish there was one). Well, the *but* was going to a rental some-where, storing the furni-ture, two moves, and how long before the ideal condo would come on the mar-ket! Okay, pay the price (fix up the joint!). It meant a roof over our heads—and there was that pool, wasn't there? If all fails, forget it and go for a dip!

The moving parties, goodbye to wonderful neighbors, only moving to another part of town but it seems like going to Zam-bi-a (where is that any-way)? Then "time like an ever-rolling stream" bears all the minutes, hours, days, nights away and that day!

The moving day arrives—"Hold back the dawn!" The truck is in the driveway (put it in gear, gal). Be strong. No neutral now; it is happening. Packers have done the job; what can't fit in the smaller space has been given away. The fifty *Hardy Boys* books collected in years of going to rummage sales, house sales, book sales, the Raggedy Ann and Andy that have absorbed lots of tears and went on the first plane ride (strapped in the seat belt) are tired but ready to go. The pictures, the awards, the law degree—the MSW, the sheets, the silverware, the blankets and beds, the frills and essentials! All now ready for the ride! What's not quite ready? Putting the car in reverse, going down the driveway for the last time, then turning around the corner! Eyes forward—no! No backward glance!

The Settle-In

What in the world! New address, new turn into the parking garage under the building, new spaces. (We get two, that's good! Looks like stanchions; we are not cattle or horses, are we?). But if we want to park, this is it! (Heated though—bet we will like it come winter?)

On the way to the elevator, we meet two new neighbors. One greets us with a smile; the other hardly speaks, grunts a hello. (Oh! Oh! He doesn't like anything new, wishes we were dead!) Something grumbles out of his thin lips: "If you people make any changes, it'll cost you."

The first elevator ride— oh, we can climb the stairs, need exercise! Keys! Need keys everywhere. Elevator won't work without a key (elevator directions: insert key, turn to the left), right? It works—*swoosh*! Big door opens, swallows you up! Up lifting, first floor! Neat, all easy, no fears! Open the condo door! Boxes everywhere, movers asking, "Where do you want this?"

And this? That's good! Nothing really looks like it did in the house. Kitchen needs paint—"Don't start that now! Hate the sick-looking car- pet!" Must have my Parquet Versailles floors; wasn't that part of the deal? (Calling that floor company at 6:00 in the a.m.!) Body too tired to think anymore. Food and sleep, all that is really needed.

We are moved in—"all in" for sure!

Then days flow into weeks and months and years, and strangely enough, this two-bedroom, two-bath condo, first floor, no-den, balcony looking over the pool has become "home." One goes in/out each day, one celebrates birthdays, one gets sick with the flu, one puts up a Christmas tree and sings "Silent Night," one laughs, one cries, one visits, one reads, one drinks tea and champagne—in fact, one lives and one finds *life in the condo*!

The Hall = The Street

Parts of the Condo

*H*alls. Halls become like the street! Once you open the door to venture forth, you are in a public area; they call it "common area." Here is where you find the garbage shoot! Here is where you go each day to get your mail. (Keys again, don't forget those keys! Heaven forbid! Major problem: no minors here!)

Halls? Yep! You are vulnerable. You can be asked, "How are you?" You really feel lousy (excuse the expression), but you must smile and say, "Fine!"

Here, you are informed of the weather! Here, you learn what happened in the night, and you were not aware of any noise. Here, the vacuum runs on Tuesdays/Thursdays. Here, you mustn't lean against the walls (common area). Here, you learn that your neighbor fell at church, broke her leg— bad with bones sticking out through the skin (isn't that a compound fracture?). Here, you learn that your other neighbors who winter in Florida—and are back early—both have cancer and want their doctors!

What's next? Here is where the paper company leaves your newspaper each morning (they come at 4:00 a.m.!). They are faithful, aren't they? And you complain if the paper is late one day!

Oh yes! The hall—the quiet days, when you wish you might see someone coming the other way. The all-too-quiet days when you lower your eyes, make

your way to the elevator,
push the button, move on—
just because there is no
other way to go!

The Elevator

This is like a "newsroom." Notices are posted; board meetings announced, time/place (must read the meeting agenda); parties are listed (first floor brings appetizers, second floor brings salads, third floor brings desserts!); death notices are put up (services, time, place); and welcome signs for the new "move-ins."

Someone likes to make notes and comments on the notices! A NO-NO! Someone likes to take down the notices (BIG NO-NO)!

What if the elevator gets stuck? There are directions for using the elevator phone, not to panic! Oh! But one day two people were stuck in the elevator! Ekk! Claustrophobia client may not apply.

Maybe the elevator is like the heart to the human body: it pumps up and down numerous times a day, it distributes the vital energy of life each hour, each day. (Oh, real vital signs?) And then when it stops? Well? Nothing! But there are rules for using the elevator: don't put it on HOLD too long, don't leave the door open (with lock on hold) to go to the mailbox, and— oh!—first stop to talk with a neighbor getting the mail. Oh, loud buzzer goes off (elevator complaint)!

The elevator is the one spot that you must speak to your neighbor! If one gets on with you, no silences! Pleasantries must be exchanged! Weather is always, always discussed!

Then one day, the elevator pads appear!

Someone moves IN or OUT. The elevator now is ready to take in the new earthly possessions or take the old out to the waiting truck in the driveway to establish a home at another address.

There are stairs, if you can climb them, or in the emergency. Thank heaven for elevators: old, new, large, small—freight or whatever!

Dear elevator, *life in the condo* would be impossible without you!

Ode to the Elevator

Creaking and Groaning,
I call—you,
From basement to
Third you go!
Please hurry, for
Me, I need you!
My bladder is "on
overflow"!

The Rules

*T*his is when things get really tough!

No one likes the rules, except when someone breaks one! *And* that someone is the person who has memorized them long ago and "spouts" them with regularity!

There are rules for almost everything: rules for garbage/recycling (keep the recycle items separate from the garbage), rules for the garage exit/ entrance (don't drive over five miles an hour! don't play with your remote!), rules for garage car washing (in fifteen years, only saw one owner washing his car!), rules for notices posted on the garage and bulletin board. There are so many rules that a *rule book* is given out at real estate closings. You are required to read and follow "the following"! Cooperation makes life easier. Question: what about smoking? True answer: *not* in the common areas. (They tried to get an amendment to ban all smoking even in the units. That failed. Owners' rights maybe?)

Rules about dogs? Oh! Oh! Now you're talking! Getting too close to the shorthairs! "Are you kidding? My dog would never do that!"

Anyway, lots of dog rules: Limited to size, thirty-five pounds. Dogs go down the stairs, must carry plastic bags for "the pickup." Dogs must *never, never* bark! (How does that happen?) Dogs are not allowed to use the front door. Dogs must be leashed at all times (even the cute ones that people *oooh* and *ahhh* over). Where? Ek, even in the elevator. Broken rule? No?

Cats? What about cats? Allowed but confined to the units. They become the silent companions!

Rules are prepared by the "god almighty" board and distributed to the owners. Democracy? What is that here? But strangely enough, they seem to work, and *life in the condo* plays on each day. And maybe, just maybe, even in spite of "the rules."

The Pool

The pool! Another world! Along about Memorial Day each year, lounge chairs come out of storage. They appear around the pool deck, and activity begins. Yeah! For the end of winter!

The pool crew appears; the pool cover is drawn back and *ekk*! The pool at this stage is NOT pretty! Some water is at the bottom, from the fall closing to keep the cement from cracking over winter, so the water looks terrible! Not to worry. In a flash, the maintenance crew has everything under control. Experts arrive, hose the sides, install the ladders, turn on the water, and before long, another glance, and new fresh streams from secret pipes appear. And yes, the happy sounds of splashing water fill the air! It's HAPPY time. SWIM time is just around the corner! Or is it? Well, no! It will take days to heat that water, more waiting time!

Strangely though, the workers and the dog walk-ers gather around the pool fence, taking wagers about when they will get the first splash of this new year! Have to wait for that water to warm up. You know how it is? These "old bones" don't like the cold!

Then very soon the notices appear on the bulletin board that, yes, indeed! THE POOL IS OPEN! There will be an "opening" pool party! Date and time? Sounds good, will plan to go this year. Wonder who is on the pool committee? That is a group that plans three parties: one when the pool opens, one midseason, and one when the pool closes.

Sometimes it is "bring a dish
to pass" party. Sometimes
it is "bring your money"
food-catered. One time,
it was a theme party, and
an impersonator of Elvis
came. He was all dressed
in white, long side burns,
sat on the ladies' laps, sang
"Love Me Tender" (oh,
joy divine!). What a night.
Then, of all things, most
unlikely, the *police* came!
They shut down the party!
Too much noise? Someone
in the neighborhood called
and complained! Too late?
(It was only 7:30 p.m.) Oh!
Well, better not do that
again! "Those crazy condo

people! They are usually so nice and quiet. Can't imagine what got into them."

Could it be just a lapse of remembrance of dancing nights? And swooning-at-Elvis days? And records playing "At Last, My Love Has Come Along" and "Sentimental Journey" and swinging out to "jukebox Saturday nights" and just lingering before dark, delaying going to the silent units alone where no one answers to a *yoo-hoo* when opening the door?

But the pool, wonderful pool! It's the center of summer, and every year, when the forsythia blooms around the pool fence, it will signal smiles and moments of anticipation, positive feelings that—yes!— as Robert Browning said, "God's in His heaven and all's right with the world." For one bright, shining moment, things are looking up! Oh! I know new faces will appear, new owners who moved in over the winter, and some old familiar faces will not be here to "sign in" as they had so often. But the sounds of summer—the splashing, the chairs moving, the chatter, the joy of jumping in the water, the cheers, the laughter, the aerobic exercise classes on Wednesdays at 9:00 a.m. with the CD playing "You Ain't Nothing But a Hound Dog" and the ladies swaying to "My Gal."

And oh yes! Let me not forget the blooming of the crab apple trees that ring the pool fence. There are all shades of pink, light and dark, and some white blossoms in between. Breezes come up to shake the limbs, happy as if they too are glad to be back after the long winter. Though the colors will fade and the green leaves will take their place, they herald the change and whisper *hope*.

The condo calendar moves; then each ever-returning spring when the pool opens—it is an event for the *life in the condo*.

The Board
(The Bored?)

$\mathcal{E}$ach year, the state requires that a board of managers be elected to run (manage), plan the condo for the coming year. Five spots are on each board, a president, a secretary, a treasurer, and two opens. Each member has a vote; majority rules. One must be an owner to be on the board. There are four required open meetings a year. All information (time/ place) posted in the elevator; all encouraged to attend. Reports are given, plans discussed, finances accounted for, and if no other issues raised during the owner's time to speak, meetings are adjourned. It all sounds quite easy. In truth, it can be difficult. There are big money matters that come before the board. It is responsible for the physical well-being of the building—things like water heaters, walks, painting, everything in the common area. It is accountable to the owners for spending the funds etc., *and* if no big controversies arise (BIG, BIG IF), life is quite pleasant.

The hardest part? The phone calls. Usually a phone call is a complaint call. "Why was such and such done? Why this? Why that?" One call came in that someone's dog had diarrhea while going through the lobby. "Didn't the board know that dogs are NOT allowed in the lobby in the first place? Who was to clean it all up? Who? Who?"

One call came in that someone had nailed new pictures to the lobby walls.

"Hate those pictures. Didn't the board know that was against the rules? My goodness!" Another call: the garage door was stuck open. "Didn't the board know the heat was going out on that zero day?" Another call: someone was taking down notices posted in the elevator and slashing other notices. (Who would do a thing like that?—childish at best.) The phone rings: someone has locked themselves out of their unit again, can't find their extra key. *Ring! Ring!* Oh no! The "condo maniac" is at it again, sprinkling pencil-sharpener shavings all down the hall! And life goes on. Maybe being on the board is not so bored and easy after all. No wonder it is quite a feat to get a new board elected each and every year. However, somehow each year it works. A required report is presented to the state, and *life in the condo* goes on.

Happenings

One day an owner on the first floor looked up to see a bikini swimsuit fly by her window and land on the bushes! Well? The vision of a naked someone dashed in her head! Very shortly, thereafter, a knock came on her door. The new owner on the third floor wondered if she happened to see her swimsuit. Turns out that the new third-floor owner had put her bikini on the balcony railing to dry (strictly and very definitely strictly against the rules!), and a breeze had come up to enforce those rules and sent the bikini off the balcony and on its downward way! Never know when you look out your window!

Another time, one of the owner's cats got out into the hall and was gaily crouching to catch, of all things, a mouse! Major upheaval in the building (an atomic bomb had exploded!) in the form of a mouse! "Is it Mildred's fault? She never takes her garbage out!"

The exterminator was summoned by presidential decree! All units were checked for evidence—those fuzzy, little, gray creatures had invaded!

Call out the guard! The cavalry! Something! Someone! This is serious!

It was fall, and they had come into the garage to get warm; they didn't know cats resided here too! Alarm! Alarm!

This was the major event of the fall season and talked about for days upon days, months upon months, and discussed in detail at the board meeting (cheese, enough already).

Finally, after much consternation, money spent, and a lecture by an expert on the life and habits of rodents (specifically mice!) explaining that mice have no bones—just ligaments, muscles, tendons or something (that is why they can squeeze into small holes, cracks, etc. [see, one can learn something new any time!])—in the end, problem solved? At least for today.

One of the owners had gone to Florida for a winter visit with her brother

and sister-in-law. She had
returned quite upset as,
while there, her brother's
dog had chewed up her
night tooth guard. It seemed
that she had put her tooth
guard on the nightstand
and turned around to find
something. This huge dog
had grabbed it from the
nightstand. The sister-in-
law wondered what those
white scraps were on the
living-room carpet? Bet
the dog had a "chewing"
feeling in its stomach?

An owner reported of
a conversation with her
sister who had moved
recently with her hus-

band into a retirement home. The sister called one day, quite excited, "They had met some new friends, a couple." After a long pause, she exclaimed, "They are both one hundred years old!" The sister noticed when looking down that the man was wearing hiking boots! Sixty-four-dollar question: Where was he going to hike? Down the hall? Or maybe just to bed?

There are large and small crises! Right? Little ones, like leaving the front door open all night or spilling food/drinks on the carpet, or revving up the cars in the garage enough to fill the air with carbon mon-oxide enough to kill thir-ty-two people!

But *then* there are big ones! Like the lady on the third floor who tried to stop the toilet from mak-ing a noise when flush-ing and decided to stuff a towel in the toilet to stop it from overflowing. Then she decided to have a glass of wine before retiring! Yup! You guessed it! The water kept going all night and by morning was flow-ing into two units below plus the meeting room! The owners awoke to a disaster! Multiple board members were called to deliberate! And so they did! What now? Cleanup crews? Insurance adjusters? Lawyers? Remodel the meeting room—no conclusion on color of the carpet? Or walls? One year later, they could use the meeting room again. The third-floor culprit had been moved out by the family—all damages repaired! Whew! That time is still referred to as "the flood." No Noah around, but two by two, the owners will never forget! New rule (no. 1,102): in case you are tempted to put towels in the toilet, THINK AGAIN! A mighty *no-no*!

Funny how humans react when cornered. Like the time a canine decided to "do its duty" before it was taken out for its walk. It didn't quite make it to the elevator! When other residents (upon using the elevator) discovered the "evidence," they called the building president, who just happened to be a dog owner. The caller made the gross error of suggesting that the canine with the digestive problem just might belong to the president! Uh-oh!

The next time some-
one exited the elevator,
the president was sitting
around the corner with his
hunting rifle (fortunately
for all, not loaded)!

A quick call to the
police, an arrest, a hear-
ing—the whole ball of wax
was executed pronto. No
harm done *but* a startling
revelation that someone
had a gun. Whew! The gos-
sip machine worked over-
time but soon faded as the
president moved away, and
no one was sorry.

The sociologists will
have to study why and
how people live together,

or haven't they been doing
that for thousands upon
thousands of years? Are
humans really any bet-
ter at it? They can't make
it alone! They follow the
crowd. They love to love
one another! They shoot
one another! They steal
one another's mates! Are
they really any better than
the Flintstones? Are they
really better than the trav-
elers who had to go through
Samaria to get to the other
side? Do they really want
to scare someone with a
gun just because they sug-
gested a dog had left its
"calling card" by the ele-

vator? Time will tell. But will it? Yes! No! Or maybe.

A sinking feeling occurs when the musical sound of an ambulance reaches your ears, and upon looking out the window, the following happens: The ambulance backs into the garage driveway. The paramedics emerge quickly. Following trained procedures, they disappear into the garage, gurney and all. One waits doing mental gymnastics— who is it? Could be Mr. So and So or maybe Mrs. ——? Saw them walking slowly last Tuesday! (Hope it isn't someone you know!) Know it is trouble for somebody. Can they please be helped? Who made the call?

Then the garage door flies up. The team and full gurney are whisked away in the waiting vehicle within moments. To where? Will they ever return? Who will be waiting at the end of the way? Basic life questions that ninety percent of the time we don't want to talk about or even think about.

One turns to the morn-ing coffee and newspaper (quieter than usual). What if I were the one in the ambulance? Turn the page, read quickly, floods in

Sam-bi-a? (Where is that place? Anyway, maybe it's Shangri-La?)

Or paradise? If I ever find it, will they dance the hula? A second cup of Java, you ask? Don't mind if I do! And the calendar signals another day in *life in the condo.*

Why in the world! You say, "Heavens to Betsy!" (Gramma always said that!) Why would someone (we'll never know who!) on the third floor, of course, threw half-empty *open* paint cans down the garbage shoot! *Splash! Splash!* Well, I guess that could be

one way to paint the inside
of the shoot! But really?

Cleanup was not cheap!
Good use of building
reserve? Well, maybe, but
that someone— think again.
(Not even one rule for that
one!)

The recycle bin is in the
garage for papers, glass,
etc. One day, when putting
newspapers in the bin, an
owner had his library book
in one hand and the news-
paper in the other hand—
you guessed it! He acci-
dently threw the library
book (which of course was
due) into the bin with the
papers. The bin had just

been emptied, and no one's arms were long enough to reach the book! One helpful (always) elderly lady was going by, wanted to be helpful, and grabbed on to the sides of the bin! She thought that she could balance on the side and reach the unfortunate book! (She had been a library volunteer for fifty years.)

The next thing! She was hollering and was balancing on her stomach, her two feet kicking in the air, her head bobbing, her face registering panic! Someone got hold of her feet to save her from falling headfirst—

breaking her neck, being recycled, squashed into the dump on Thursday (weekly pickup day)!

Since that didn't work, an enterprising bystander opened his car trunk, took out numerous golf clubs—a try to get under the help-less library book—dragged it to the surface, and saved the day! It worked! Used a seven iron! A good approach club, now a res-cue club! The book was returned to the safety of the library with its new chap-ter—"Once upon a time, I was almost recycled"—and made it on time! The fine of ten cents a day was avoided!

Rumors began floating around the stratosphere that an owner's sister had a new boyfriend! She was eighty-five years young, and he was only ninety-two! They had met in the checkout line at the Jewel! No one seemed to know if it was the express lane (probably should have been)! Anyway, it was interesting, the number of people that were stopping at the Jewel—broke a record, I heard!

(Hmmm, wonder which Jewel that was?)

And then I guess every-
one has the good days and
bad days, like the little
lady who was commanding
all attention at the mail-
boxes! It seemed her day
had started out about as
usual, except she realized
that the shot the doctor had
given her for back pain was
supposed to be working by
now, and she just realized
it wasn't! When the phone
rang, it was her daughter,
who was quite upset. It had
rained buckets all night,
and when she opened
the basement door in the
morning, she saw things
floating like electric train

sets, clothes, Christmas ornaments, and a bottle of wine—saved because it was on a table! A table that also was floating!

Her husband went downstairs only to find the water (plus whatever else the neighbor had eaten the night before) was up to his neck! (And he was six feet tall!) It really wasn't a "red-letter" day? Then she turned on her computer only to find a notice that there was someone in Venezuela tracking her credit card, knew her vital statistics (five feet two, eyes blue). She didn't even speak Spanish (only had two lessons at the senior center). *Buenos dias, señora*! Then to end her day, she couldn't find her cellphone! Looking! Looking! Finally, there it was—fell out of her pocket! On the toilet seat! Oh well! The sun also rises.

Unwelcome Sounds

*D*ay or night, the sound of the ambulance approaching gives pause, chills, and facial wonderment signs. Where are they going? Who's next? Haven't seen him/her of late! Then the silence as one stands to watch the paramedics go into action. Wonderful, aren't they? Quick at their tasks of opening up the ambulance back door, dragging out the gurney, hustling up to the building like some guest? Anxious to see the poor soul—maybe a fall? Maybe someone stuck in the Jacuzzi tub? Maybe a heart attack? Maybe someone can't breathe? Silence. Then sooner than one could imagine, the someone is out of the doors into the waiting "mercy chariot," speeding to the HOPE HOSPITAL with lights flashing. And you wonder? Give thanks that they missed you this time!

BUT! Fun things happen too! The note in the elevator says "Breakfast at the Beach!" (date/time free bus/sign-up). Sounds good, 9:00 a.m. That's not too early, is it? There will be coffee, rolls, eggs, maybe some music to help it all go down better! Many sign up! Oh! Oh! My calendar shows a conflict, but what the heck? Smile to know that others will enjoy a beautiful, perfect morning—not eating alone today and smiling, laughing together. Just being part of the group. Not bad, I'd say. Good! Keep smiling, even dancing. Beat the clock! The old wristwatch can stay in the dresser drawer for today! Don't self-help books tell us to "live in the moment"? Well! It's a really livin' moment—at the beach!

Musings

*A*nd then one day, many times NOT with previous notification! The time will come when you moved in as a couple, and you now are a single.

The time ran out for one of you; the heart became too tired (like the *Little Red Wagon*). It said, "Enough already," ran down, and stopped! It had done its job. "Well done, thou good and faithful servant." And now what?

The drill, the routine, the procedure starts. Telephone calls to family, friends, and church. Arrangements! Arrangements! You know. How many times have you read it in the newspaper? "Too bad," you said. *Now* it is your turn. It's personal! How do you know what that means?

The church calls, wants to know what hymn to choose for the service.

You think. Yes, of course!

You pause. You know?
The strains of the organ
will sound. All will stand.
The music starts, with
notes reflecting from the
beautiful stained glass windows (that you have loved
so long).

The words will float up
to the rafters and fill the
sanctuary. With "bended
knee and heart," you hear,

The Navy Hymn—
His Favorite from
Pt Boat Days!

"Eternal Father,
strong to save,

Whose arm hath bound
the restless wave.
Who bidd'st the
mighty ocean deep,
its own appointed
limits keep.
Oh! Hear us when
we cry to thee,
for those in peril
on the sea."

Now! Just how do you
think you'll get through
that? Truth be told, you
probably won't!

But it's your turn. Time
to smile through your tears,
shake hands with some,
hug others, see so many
faces—some you have not

seen for years that stab your memory and your heart! That they came so far, that they remembered, that they cared!

Somehow, with enough arms/hands holding you, it was over, and some said, "This too will pass," and the blur goes on—the mornings being even more empty than the nights, and the clock ticks, and the pages of the calendars turn. *And* somehow, someway, one foot does go in front of the other. But you are thankful to be in the condo. It is per-fect now—almost too much space for one. Then the sympathy cards are stuck in your door or posted with your name by the mailbox. The smiles, the greetings, the "thinking of you" are exchanged in the hall, the elevator, the garage. Even by so many that have been this way before you, you look at them—you know that *they* made it to today, and you borrow some strength from them. And you wonder, now who will help you fold the sheets when they come out of the dryer? You know, this new life, this new circumstance, must be accepted.

This new strange, too quiet, scary, challenging, hopeful—yes, thankful life will go on, completing your number of days, sharing the wisdom of time and experience (counting blessings!).

Is this all there is? And you remember Peggy Lee singing:

> "If that's all
> there is? My
> friend?
>
> Then let's
> keep dancing."
>
> Is there a
> residue? A
> leftover?

A remaining?
And you can
answer YES!

And the
mission?

Pass it on!

What does that
mean? What
does one pass
on?

The *love*—that overworked, hard-to-define, impossible-to-define word—is the answer. It is the one you feel:

1. It is the one in the "inner sanctum" of your soul.
2. The energy.
3. The transforming agent (like ink in water).

4. It is the mysterious companion who has been with you from day one.
5. It is the ultimate healer.
6. The world's "precious ointment."
7. The soul's citadel.

And?
At the condo?
It's life.

24/7/365

CPSIA information can be obtained
at www.ICGtesting.com
Printed in the USA
BVHW090625091019
560603BV00004B/43/P